INVESTIGATIONS

ROCKS AND MINERALS

JACK CHALLONER & RODNEY WALSHAW

LORENZ BOOKS

First published in 2000 by Lorenz Books

© 2000 Anness Publishing Limited

Lorenz Books is an imprint of
Anness Publishing Limited
Hermes House
88–89 Blackfriars Road
London SE1 8HA

Published in the USA by Lorenz Books, Anness Publishing, Inc.,
27 West 20th Street, New York, NY 10011, (800) 354-9657

This edition distributed in Canada by
Raincoast Books, 8680 Cambie Street,
Vancouver, British Columbia V6P 6M9

A CIP catalogue record for this book is available
from the British Library

ISBN 0 7548 0457 7

Publisher: Joanna Lorenz
Managing Editor, Children's Books: Gilly Cameron Cooper
Project Editor: Joanne Hanks
Consultants: Dr Sue Bowler, Dr Bob Symes
Photographers: John Freeman, Don Last
Stylist: Melanie Williams
Designer: Caroline Grimshaw, Ann Samuel
Picture Researcher: Caroline Brooke, Daniella Marceddu
Illustrators: Peter Bull Art Studio, Guy Smith

1 3 5 7 9 10 8 6 4 2

The publishers would like to thank:
Our models: Mitchell Collins, Ashley Cronin, Louise Gannon, Hamal
Gohil, Sarah Kenna, Catherine McAlpine, Griffiths Nipah, Goke Omolena,
Ben Patrick, Anastasia Pryer, Charlie Rawlings and Victoria Wallace.
Also: Mr. and Mrs. G. R. Evans, Ian Kirkpatrick.
A special thank you to Gregory, Bottley and Lloyd for
their efficient help in supplying rock and mineral samples.

ROCKS AND MINERALS

CONTENTS

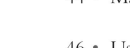

ROCKS AND MINERALS

Rocks and minerals are the naturally occurring materials that make up planet Earth. We can see them all around us—in mountains, cliffs, river valleys, beaches and quarries. Rocks are used for buildings, and many minerals are prized as jewels. Most people think of rocks as hard and heavy, but soft materials, such as sand, chalk and clay, are also considered to be rocks.

Minerals make up a part of rocks in the way that separate ingredients make a cake. About 3,500 different minerals are known to exist, but only a few hundred of these are common. Most minerals are solid but a few are liquid or gas. Water, for example, is a liquid mineral, and many other minerals are found in liquid petroleum.

You might think that rocks last for ever, but they do not. Slowly, over thousands, even millions, of years they are naturally recycled, and the minerals that occur in a rock are moved from one place to another and form new rock.

Gemstones
Minerals prized for their beauty and rarity are called gemstones. The brilliant sparkle of a diamond appears when it is carefully cut and polished (as above).

pyrite

kyanite

copper

yellow sulfur crystals growing on kaolin

opal in ironstone

Minerals
All rocks are made up of one or more minerals. Minerals are natural, solid, nonliving substances. Five different minerals are shown here. Each one has definite characteristics, such as its shape and color, that distinguish it from all other minerals. Many types of minerals are found in thousands of different types of rock.

The Earth's crust

The Earth's surface is a thin, hard, rocky shell called the crust. There are two kinds of crust—oceanic crust (under the oceans) and continental crust (the land). The recycling of the rocks that form the crust has been going on for 4,000 million years.

granite

sandstone

At some places in the hot parts of the Earth beneath the crust, huge pockets of molten rock or magma form. The magma rises, cools and solidifies to form igneous rocks such as granite. If magma reaches the surface of the Earth, it erupts as lava.

Sedimentary rocks, such as this sandstone, form from the fragments of other rocks that have been broken down by the action of rain, snow, ice and air. The fragments are carried away by wind or water and settle in a different place.

gneiss

Sometimes, within the Earth, the heat and pressure become so strong that the rocks twist and buckle and new minerals grow in them. The new rocks are called metamorphic rocks. This gneiss is a good example.

Fossils

As the fragments of rock settle in their eventual resting place, they may bury the animals and plants that lived there. The remains then become preserved as fossils. This ammonite was once a living creature, but is now made entirely of minerals.

Crystals

Minerals usually grow in regular shapes called crystals. When mineral-rich water fills a crack or cavity in a rock, veins and geodes may form. A geode is a rounded rock with a hollow center lined with crystals. The beautiful crystal lining is revealed when it is split open. Geodes are highly prized by mineral collectors.

Getting at rocks

We use rocks in many ways, but getting them out of the ground can be difficult. Explosives are often used to blast rocks out of cliff faces. Here limestone is being blasted from a quarry. Above the quarry face, large machines have been used to drill a line of holes into the ground. The holes are packed with explosives, which are detonated from far away.

LOOKING AT ROCKS

T HE best way to learn about rocks and minerals is to look closely at as many different types as you can find. Look at pebbles on the beach and the stones in your garden. You will find that they are not all the same. Collect a specimen of each different rock type and compare them with each other. Give each rock a number to identify it, and keep a record of where you found it and what you can see in each piece.

A magnifying glass will magnify your rocks and help you see details that cannot be easily seen with the naked eye. To find out how many different minerals there are in each of your specimens, look for different colors, shapes and hardness. Testing the properties of minerals, such as hardness, can help to identify what sort of rock it is. Ask an adult to take you to the nearest geological museum to compare it with the specimens there. Why not start your own museum at home or at school?

A closer look

Clean a rock with a stiff brush and water. Stand so that plenty of light shines on the rock, and experiment to find the correct distance from the hand lens to the rock.

chisel

geological hammer

safety glasses

magnifying glass

pencils

hard hat

backpack

pocketknife

notebook

water

camera

gloves

field guide

compass

bucket

collecting bags and labels

map, mark on the map the places where you found your best specimens

newspapers, for wrapping your specimens in

Rock collecting

Here is the essential equipment that you will need for collecting rocks. Wear protective clothing, and always take an adult with you when you are away from home. Safety glasses will protect your eyes from razor-sharp splinters when hammering rocks. Do not strike cliffs or quarry faces with your hammer, but stick to blocks that have already fallen. Always remember that cliffs can be very dangerous—a hard hat or helmet will protect your head from falling rocks. Do not be greedy when collecting. Rocks and minerals need protecting just as much as wildlife, and some sites are protected by law. If you are collecting on a beach with cliffs behind, be careful not to be cut off by the tide.

TESTING FOR HARDNESS

You will need: *several rock samples, bowl of water, nail brush, coin, glass jar, steel file, sandpaper.*

1 Clean some rock samples with water using a nail brush. Scratch the rocks together. On the Mohs scale, a mineral is harder than any minerals it can make scratches on.

2 A fingernail has a hardness of just over 2. Scratch each rock with a fingernail—if it scratches the rock, the minerals of which the rock is made have a hardness of 2 or less.

The hardest natural mineral is diamond, with a hardness of 10. It will scratch all other minerals.

3 Set aside those rocks scratched by a fingernail. Scratch those remaining with a coin. A coin has a hardness of about 3, so minerals it scratches are less than 3.

4 Scratch the remaining rocks on a glass jar. If any scratch the jar, then the minerals they contain must be harder than glass.

THE MOHS SCALE

• Mineral hardness is measured on a scale devised in 1822 by Friedrich Mohs. He listed ten common minerals running from 1, the softest, (talc) to 10, the hardest, (diamond).

5 Set aside any rocks that will not scratch the glass. Try scratching the remainder with a steel file (hardness 7) and finally with a sheet of sandpaper (hardness 8).

WHAT ARE MINERALS?

MINERALS are natural chemical substances that are present in all rocks. Most minerals are solid, but a few are liquid. Some minerals, such as sulfur and gold, are single elements. Others are made up of two or more elements. All rocks are a mixture of minerals. The igneous rock basalt, for example, which makes up most of Earth's oceanic crust, is a mixture of the minerals feldspar and pyroxene. Feldspar itself is a compound of oxygen, silicon and aluminum with various other elements. Silicates are the largest group of rock-forming minerals, all of which include silicon and oxygen. Quartz (the most common mineral in the Earth's crust) is a silicate. The minerals inside a rock usually form small crystal grains that are locked together to form a hard solid.

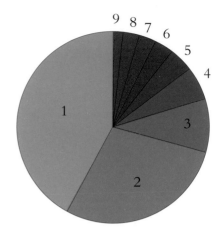

Just eight elements make up almost all minerals on Earth. Starting with the most common first, they are oxygen (1), silicon (2), aluminum (3), iron (4), calcium (5), sodium (6), potassium (7) and magnesium (8). All other elements make up (9).

Rock-forming minerals

Granite is one of the most common rocks found in the Earth's land crust. It is made mostly of quartz and feldspar with smaller amounts of mica and hornblende. As molten rock in the Earth's crust cools, the minerals form crystals and interlock with each other. Feldspar crystals are the first to crystallize and may be larger and more perfect in shape than the other minerals, which crystallize later. Feldspar is light (often pink) in color and quartz is gray and glassy. Mica is dark and silvery, while hornblende is usually jet black. Different granites have different amounts of each mineral, which is why granite varies in color from gray to reddish-pink.

mica

hornblende

granite

feldspar

quartz

Pure gold

A few minerals occur as single elements. A single element is one that is not combined with any other element. Gold is a good example of a single element. The mineral gold originally comes from hot rocks buried deep underground. Water flows through the hot rocks and dissolves the gold. Sometimes this water moves up toward the Earth's surface, cooling as it does. At lower temperatures the dissolved gold starts to harden and crystallizes into the solid form seen here.

gold

emerald in mass of mica-schist

Single element

Diamonds grow under extreme pressure deep in the Earth and are carried to the surface in a rare volcanic rock known as kimberlite. The mineral diamond contains a single element, which is carbon.

Real versus synthetic

Gemstones such as diamonds and emeralds are rare and expensive. Today, the finest quality emeralds are found in the mountains of Colombia and Brazil, in South America.

synthetic emerald

Colorful minerals

Under a microscope, a rock's crystals appear large enough to study. Scientists can identify the minerals by using filters that make polarized light. This gives each mineral its own range of colors.

Man-made crystals

Synthetic crystals can be made to grow in a particular size and shape, for a specific purpose. This is done by subjecting the crystals of more common minerals to carefully-controlled temperature and pressure. Some are used in the electronics industry for making computer chips. Others are manufactured for use in jewelry, such as the synthetic emerald cluster above.

CRYSTALS

pyrite

selenite

quartz

topaz

calcite

Most minerals found in rocks are in crystal form. They are highly prized for their beautiful colors and because they sparkle in the light. Crystals have often been associated with magic—the fortune teller's crystal ball was originally made from very large crystals of quartz. Most precious gemstones, including diamonds and rubies, are crystals.

Igneous rocks are usually made of interlocking crystals that form as hot magma (liquid rock) cools. The largest and best crystals are found in rock features known as veins. Veins are formed when hot, mineralized water rises up through the Earth. As the water cools, crystals form. Crystals may also grow when water on the Earth's surface evaporates. Each mineral variety forms crystals with a characteristic shape.

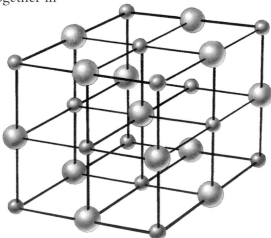

Salt magnified
These grains of ordinary table salt, seen under a powerful microscope, grew when salt water was evaporated. The grains are minute crystals, each containing billions of tiny particles known as atoms. The grains of salt are shaped like tiny cubes because of the way the atoms are arranged inside them. Each variety of mineral forms crystals with an individual shape.

Inside crystals
The shape of a crystal is controlled by the way that the atoms inside it are arranged. Imagine that the oranges in these boxes are atoms. In the left box the atoms are stacked in a disorderly way. Atoms that join like this do not produce crystals. Instead, they produce a material called glass. In a crystal, atoms join together in an orderly way, as in the box on the right.

Crystal faces
Crystals sparkle because their surfaces, or faces, reflect the light. Each individual mineral or group of minerals has faces that are always at the same angles relative to each other. There are seven main groups of crystals based on the arrangements of faces. The mineral crystals shown here illustrate five of the different groups.

The crystal lattice
The atoms in a crystal link together to form a three-dimensional framework known as the crystal lattice. This repeats itself in all directions as the crystal grows, giving the crystal its regular shape and controlling the angles between the faces. This picture shows ordinary salt or halite. The green balls represent chlorine atoms, the blue ones are sodium.

*reniform,
hematite*

*lamellar,
muscovite mica*

*rosette, gypsum
(desert rose)*

acicular, pyrite

How does your crystal grow?

A mineral's habit is the shape in which its crystals grow. Different habits form according to the conditions in which crystals grow. Each habit is the result of the crystal lattice framework growing more in some directions than others. A selection of habits is shown here. Each habit has a different name that describes the way it looks. *Acicular* are needle-like crystals, *lamellar* means paper thin, *reniform* are kidney-shaped, and *dendritic* are tree-like.

*fibrous,
cockscomb
barite*

*acicular, gypsum
(daisy gypsum)*

dendritic, manganese oxide

prismatic, amethyst

Crystal colors

The color of a crystal in natural light is a useful aid to identifying its mineral. Many types of mineral have characteristic colors, but several occur in a variety of colors. Quartz, for example, can be white, gray, red, purple, pink, yellow, green, brown, black and colorless. Citrine, rock crystal and rose quartz are three types of quartz. Amethyst is purple quartz.

citrine

*rock
crystal*

*rose
quartz*

Crystal twins

Sometimes crystals form so that two (or more) seem to intergrow symmetrically with each other. These are called twin crystals. Aragonite *(above)* often grows twinned crystals.

MAKING CRYSTALS

Most solid substances, including metals, consist of crystals. To see how crystals form, think what happens when sugar is put into hot water. The sugar dissolves to form a solution. If you take the water away again, the sugar molecules are left behind and join to reform into crystals. See this happen for yourself by trying the project below. Crystals can also form as a liquid cools. The type of crystals that form will depend on which substances are dissolved in the liquid. In a liquid, the atoms or molecules are loosely joined together. They can move around, which is why a liquid flows. As the liquid solidifies, the molecules do not move around so much and will join together, usually to form a crystal. You can see this if you put a drop of water on a mirror and leave it in a freezer overnight. Finally, make a simple goniometer (a device used to measure the angles between the faces of some objects).

Ice crystals
A drop of water placed on a dry mirror will spread out a little, then freeze solid in the freezer. Examine the crystals that form with a magnifying glass.

You will need: water, measuring cup, saucepan, sugar, tablespoon, wooden spoon, glass jar.

GROWING CRYSTALS

1 Ask an adult to heat half a quart of water in a saucepan until it is hot, but not boiling. Using a tablespoon, add sugar to the hot water until it will no longer dissolve.

2 Stir the solution well, then let it cool. When it is quite cold, pour the solution from the pan into a glass jar and put it somewhere where it will not be disturbed.

3 After a few days or weeks, the sugar in the solution will gradually begin to form crystals. The longer you leave it, the larger your crystals will grow.

MAKING A GONIOMETER

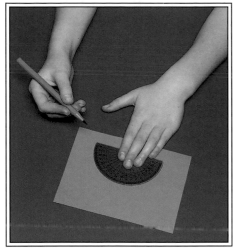

1 Firmly hold a protractor on a piece of card stock. Draw carefully around the protractor onto the card stock using a dark felt-tip pen or soft pencil. Do not move the protractor.

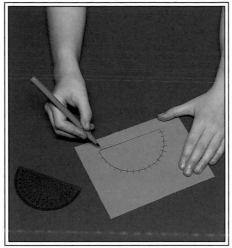

2 With the protractor still in place, mark off 10-degree divisions around the edge. Remove the protractor and then mark the divisions inside the semicircle.

3 Cut out the semicircle. Now cut a thin strip of card stock about one inch longer than the base of your semicircle. Cut one end square and cut the other end into a point.

You will need: *protractor, two pieces of card stock, felt-tipped pen or pencil, scissors, ruler, paper fastener.*

Measuring the angles

People who study crystals sometimes use a device called a goniometer. It measures the angles between the faces of a crystal. The angle can help to identify a mineral.

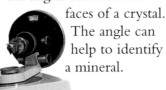

a simple goniometer

4 Make holes in the pointer and semicircle big enough for the paper fastener, and attach them with the fastener as shown. Flatten out the fastener on the back.

5 Collect some objects with straight sides or faces. Rest the straight face of your semicircle on one face of the object. Move the blunt end of your pointer onto the next face. The other end will point on the scale to the angle between the faces. Real goniometers are more complex and accurate than this, but they measure angles in a similar way to your homemade one and help to identify minerals.

IGNEOUS ROCKS

IGNEOUS rocks start off deep within the Earth as magma (molten rock). The name igneous means "of fire." The magma rises toward the surface where it may erupt as lava from a volcano, or cool and solidify within the Earth's crust. Igneous rocks that extrude, or push out, above ground are called extrusive. Those that solidify underground are called intrusive. Igneous rocks are a mass of interlocking crystals, which makes them very strong and ideal as building stones.

The size of the crystals depends on how quickly the magma cooled. Lavas cool quickly and contain very small crystals. Intrusive rocks cool much more slowly and have much larger crystals. The most common kind of lava, basalt, makes up most of the Earth's oceanic crust. Granite is a common intrusive igneous rock. It forms huge plugs, up to several miles thick and just as wide, in the continental crust. These are called plutons. They are often found under high mountains such as the Alps or the Himalayas.

Microscopic view
Geologists look at rocks under a special kind of microscope that shows the minerals in the rock. This is what an igneous rock called dolerite looks like. Notice the way the crystals fit together with no spaces between. Dolerite is a volcanic lava that formed beneath the ground. It has larger crystals than extrusive basalt.

Fine-grained granite
The magma that makes granite below the ground can also erupt at the surface. This Stone Age ax is made of a lava called rhyolite, and has razor-sharp edges. Its crystals are tiny.

Coarse-grained granite
This sample of granite is typical of igneous rocks. The large crystals give the rock a grainy texture. The crystals are large because they grew slowly as the liquid magma cooled down slowly.

Fine-grained basalt
Basalt is the most common extrusive igneous rock, especially in the oceanic crust. Basalt cools much more quickly than granite, so the crystals are smaller and the rock looks and feels smoother.

Glassy obsidian
When magma cools very rapidly, the atoms or molecules are not able to join together in a regular pattern to form crystals. Instead, they form a glass-like amorphous (without distinct shape) material, such as this obsidian. This rock has the same composition as granite and rhyolite, but there are no crystals.

Half dome

Millions of years ago, a huge dome of magma intruded under what is now Yosemite National Park in California. It slowly cooled to form granite. Over a period of time, the rocks around it were worn away by glaciers, exposing these dome-shaped hills of granite behind.

Granite tors

On Dartmoor in the southwest of England are the remains of large granite plutons that solidified below a chain of mountains. The mountains were eroded away, but the granite, being hard and weather-resistant, remains to form shapes known as tors. They look like huge boulders stacked on top of each other.

Rivers of liquid basalt

The islands of Hawaii are the exposed tops of huge piles of basalt that is still erupting after many thousands of years. The hot lava glows red in the dark and is capable of flowing for several miles before solidifying. Parts of Scotland and Ireland looked like this about 50 million years ago.

As the lava of the Giant's Causeway cooled, it cracked into interlocking, six-sided columns of basalt rock.

Giant's Causeway

The impressive columns of the Giant's Causeway in Northern Ireland are solid basalt. As lava reached the surface, it flowed into the sea, where it cooled and split into mainly hexagonal (six-sided) columns. The minerals that make up basalt, such as feldspars, pyroxenes and olivine, typically give the rock a dark-gray to black color.

MAKING IGNEOUS ROCKS

T HE projects on these pages will show you how igneous rocks can be grainy and made of large crystals, or smooth and glassy. You will be melting sugar and then letting it solidify. Sugar melts at a low enough temperature for you to experiment with it safely at home. To make real magma, you would need to heat pieces of rock up to around 1,832°F until it melted! Even with sugar, the temperature must be high, so ask an adult to help you while you are carrying out these projects. You can also make the sugar mixture into bubbly "honeycomb" candy, which is similar in form to the rock pumice. It is like pumice because hundreds of tiny bubbles are captured inside the hot sugar.

"honeycomb" candy (pumice)

toffee (obsidian)

fudge (granite)

Fudge's grainy texture is similar to granite. Like obsidian, glassy toffee cools too rapidly to form crystals. The bubbles in "honeycomb" candy are like pumice.

You will need: *sugar, water, saucepan, safety glasses, wooden spoon, milk.*

MAKING CRYSTALLINE ROCK

1 Ask an adult to heat about 16 oz (1 lb) of sugar with a little water in a pan. Continue heating until the mixture turns brown, but not black, then add a dash of milk.

2 Let the mixture in the pan cool to room temperature. After an hour, you should see tiny crystal grains in the fudge mixture. Once it is completely cool, feel its texture.

MAKING GLASS AND BUBBLES

1 Use waxed paper to spread the butter on a metal baking sheet. Put in the freezer for at least an hour to get cold. Use oven mitts to take the sheet from the freezer.

2 Ask an adult to heat about 16 oz (1 lb) of sugar with a little water in a saucepan. The sugar dissolves in the water, but the water soon evaporates, leaving only sugar.

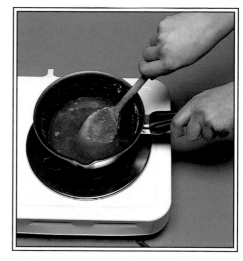

3 Stir the sugar mixture with a wooden spoon while it is heating. Make sure that the sugar does not burn and turn black. It should be golden brown.

Baking soda gives off the gas carbon dioxide to form tiny bubbles.

You will need: *waxed paper, butter, baking sheet, oven mitts, sugar, water, saucepan, wooden spoon, safety glasses, baking soda.*

5 To make "honeycomb" candy, stir in a spoonful of baking soda in Step 3, just before you pour the sugar onto the sheet. This will make tiny bubbles of gas in your "magma."

4 Pour the mixture onto the cool baking sheet. After 10 minutes, the glassy and brittle toffee will be cool enough to pick up.

SEDIMENTARY ROCKS

MANY of the most familiar rocks that we see around us are sedimentary rocks. Particles of rock, minerals and the shells and bones of sea creatures, settle in layers and then harden into rock over thousands of years. Rock particles form when other rocks are eroded (worn down) by the weather and are carried away by wind, rivers or ice sheets. They become sediments when they are dumped and settle. Sediments may collect in areas such as river deltas, lakes and the sea. Very large particles make conglomerates (large pebbles cemented together), medium-sized ones make sandstones and very fine particles make clays. Some sediments are made entirely of seashells. Others form when water evaporates to form a deposit called evaporite. Rock salt is a sedimentary rock and is used to make table salt.

Sandstone monolith
Uluru (Ayers Rock) is a monolith (single block of stone) in central Australia. It is the remains of a vast sandstone formation that once covered the entire region.

Clay
The particles in clay are too fine even to see with a microscope. Clay absorbs water, which makes it pliable and useful for modeling.

Limestone
This is one of the most common sedimentary rocks. It forms in water and consists mainly of the mineral calcite. Rainwater will dissolve it.

Conglomerate
A conglomerate contains rounded pebbles cemented together by rock made of much smaller particles.

Chalk
Chalk is made from the skeletons of millions of tiny sea creatures. The white cliffs of Dover on the southern coast of England are chalk.

Sandstone
There are many types and colors of sandstone. Each different type is made of tiny grains joined together. The grains are usually quartz.

Red sandstone
The quartz grains in this rock are coated with the mineral hematite (iron oxide) to give the red color. The rock is from an ancient desert.

Old and new

This cliff, on the coast of Dorset, in southern England, is made of layers of hard limestone and soft mudstone. Both rocks were once at the bottom of a shallow tropical sea at a time when dinosaurs roamed on land. The sea was teeming with all kinds of creatures that were buried and became fossils. The cliff is falling (making it dangerous) and will make new sediment as it is broken up by the waves and carried into the sea.

Beach pebbles

To see how the particles in sedimentary rocks form, look at the different sizes of pebbles on a beach. The constant back and forth of the waves grinds the pebbles smaller and smaller. When they settle and the conditions are right, these particles will form sedimentary rock.

Meeting place

Many sedimentary rocks form at deltas, where a river meets the sea. The river's flow slows right down, so sediment can no longer be carried in the water and is deposited. This picture of a delta on the island of Madagascar was taken from a satellite.

Rock salt pillars

The salt that forms rock salt is a chemical compound called sodium chloride, or halite. Rock salt forms as water evaporates from a salt solution, such as sea water. Here, pillars have formed in the extremely salty water of the Dead Sea, on the border between Israel and Jordan.

The red color of this halite is caused by impurities.

As water dries out, rock salt forms in pillars at the lake's edge.

FACT BOX

• Sedimentary rocks are said to be lithified, which means turned to stone. The word comes from the Greek word *lithos* (stone). The solid part of the Earth (including the crust) is called the lithosphere.

• Large areas of the world are covered with a yellow sedimentary rock called loess. The word comes from an old German word meaning loose. This is because loess consists of tiny dust particles that settled after being blown long distances by the wind.

ROCKS IN LAYERS

Strata sandwich
A multi-layer sandwich is like rock strata. The first layer is a slice of bread at the bottom. Each filling is laid on top with more slices of bread. When it is cut through you can see the many different layers.

SEDIMENTARY rocks form as small particles of rock accumulate at the bottom of seas and lakes, or in deserts. These particles settle to cover large areas and, over thousands or millions of years, new layers of sediment are laid down on top of existing ones.

As a result, most sedimentary rocks form in layers, called strata. The strata that are deepest underground are the oldest, because more recent layers are laid down on top of them. For this reason, sedimentary rock strata can provide valuable clues about the distant history of the Earth.

Once formed, sedimentary rocks may be subject to powerful forces caused by the movement of the Earth's crust. The forces squeeze the strata into folds and crack them. Along some large cracks, known as faults, blocks of rock slide past each other. Both folds and faults are often clearly visible in rock faces.

Folded strata
This rock face shows what happens when parts of the Earth's crust are pushed together in a collision zone. Geologists call downward folds synforms and upward folds antiforms. Folds are found in many sizes, from the microscopic to the gigantic. Mountain ranges have very large folds, sometimes with strata turned upside down. Old rocks may have been folded many times.

Layers of rock
Rock faces in cliffs, river valleys and mountains reveal sedimentary rock. Here you can see different layers of the same rock repeated. The layers are not of equal thickness. This suggests that conditions in this region changed many times in the past. Unequal thicknesses are common in layers of sediment found deposited at the mouths of large rivers.

Geological time chart

Era	Period	Million years ago
Cenozoic	**Quaternary**	
	Holocene (epoch)	0.01
	Pleistocene (epoch)	2
	Tertiary	
	Pliocene (epoch)	5
	Miocene (epoch)	25
	Oligocene (epoch)	38
	Eocene (epoch)	55
	Paleocene (epoch)	65
Mesozoic	**Cretaceous**	144
	Jurassic	213
	Triassic	248
Paleozoic	**Permian**	286
	Carboniferous	360
	Devonian	408
	Silurian	438
	Ordovician	505
	Cambrian	590
Pre-Cambrian		4,600

Layers of seashells
In some sedimentary rocks there are layers made mostly of shells. In this picture the rock has split along the shell layer. It is like looking at the filling in a sandwich from above, after the top slice of bread has been removed.

Rocks and time
To put events in their correct place in time, it is necessary to have a framework or calendar that divides time in a way that is understood by everyone. Geologists have devised their own special calendar that is known as the Geological Timescale. This calendar starts 4,600 million years ago, which is the date of the oldest known rocks people have discovered. In this calendar, there are four major subdivisions, known as Eras. These are subdivided into Periods and Epochs (as shown in the chart above). So if you tell someone that you have found a Miocene fossil, he or she will know how old it is by referring to the calendar.

Clues to the past
Layers of sedimentary rock sometimes look different from each other. The differences are often evidence of climate changes in the past. Other differences might have been caused by the movement of tectonic plates.

Grand Canyon
The bottom strata of the 1-mile deep Grand Canyon, in Arizona is more than 2,000 million years old. Those at the top are about 60 million years old.

MAKING SEDIMENTARY ROCKS

To help you understand the processes by which sedimentary rocks are made and how they form distinct layers called strata, you can make your own sedimentary rocks. Different strata of rock are laid down by different types of sediment, so the first project involves making strata of your own, using various things found around the kitchen. The powerful forces that move parts of the Earth's crust often cause strata to fold, fault or just tilt and you can see this, too. In the second project, you can make a copy of a type of sedimentary rock called a conglomerate, in which small pebbles and sand become cemented into a finer material. Conglomerates in nature can be found in areas that were once under water.

The finished jar with its layers imitates real rock strata. Most sediments are laid down flat, but the forces that shape the land may tilt them, as here.

You will need:
large jar, modeling clay, spoon, flour, kidney beans, brown sugar, rice, lentils (or a similar variety of ingredients of different colors and textures).

YOUR OWN STRATA

1 Press one edge of a large jar into a piece of modeling clay, so that the jar sits at an angle. Slowly and carefully spoon a layer of flour about 1 inch thick into the jar.

2 Carefully add layers of kidney beans, brown sugar, rice, lentils and flour, building them up until they almost reach the top of the jar. Try to keep the side of the jar clean.

3 Remove the jar from the clay and stand it upright. The different colored and textured layers are like a section through a sequence of natural sedimentary rocks.

MAKING CONGLOMERATE ROCK

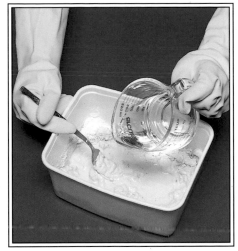

1 Put on a pair of rubber gloves. In a container, mix up some plaster of Paris with water, following the instructions on the package.

2 Mix some small pebbles, sand and soil into the plaster of Paris. Stir the mixture thoroughly to make sure they are all evenly distributed.

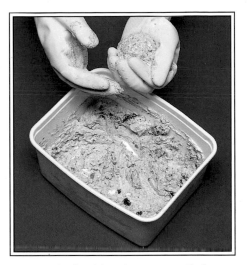

3 Let sit for 10 minutes, until the mixture starts to harden, then mold a small lump of it into a ball in your hand.

finished rocks

You will need:
rubber gloves, old plastic container, plaster of Paris, water, fork or spoon, pebbles, sand, soil, paper.

4 Make some more conglomerate rocks in different sizes with different amounts of pebbles. Place the rocks on a piece of paper to harden and dry out completely.

The real thing
Do your rocks look anything like this boulder of real conglomerate rock? The many fragments in this boulder vary a great deal in size and color.

METAMORPHIC ROCKS

THE word metamorphic means "changed," and that is exactly what these rocks are. Metamorphic rocks form when igneous or sedimentary rocks are subjected to high temperatures or are crushed by huge pressures underground. Such forces change the properties and the appearance of the rocks. For example, the sedimentary rock limestone becomes marble, which has a different texture and new minerals that are not found in the original limestone.

There are two types of metamorphism. In contact metamorphism, hot magma heats the surrounding rocks and changes them. In regional metamorphism, deeper rocks are changed when sections of the Earth's crust collide. In the intense heat and pressure of these collision zones the rocks start to melt in some places, new minerals appear and the layers are pushed into strange shapes.

contact aureole

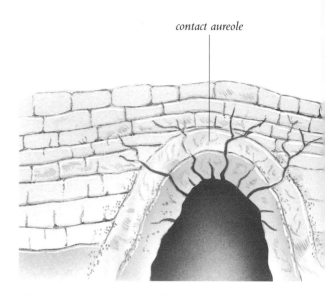

Contact metamorphism
This type of metamorphism occurs when an intrusion of magma bakes the rocks surrounding it. The zone of rock surrounding the magma is called a contact aureole. The magma alters the form and composition of the rocks. The changes are most noticeable close to the intrusion and gradually become less obvious farther away.

Mica crystals in slate give it a shiny, wet appearance.

The minerals form in bands, giving a foliated (layered) appearance.

The mineral olivine gives this marble its green color. The rest is mostly calcite.

Slate
This rock is formed from mudstone or shale, sedimentary rocks containing tiny particles of clay. Slate forms under very high pressure, but at a relatively low temperature. Because of this, fossils from the original rocks are often preserved but may be squeezed out of shape by the pressure.

Gneiss
Under very high temperature and pressure, many igneous or sedimentary rocks can become gneiss (pronounced "nice"). All gneisses are made of layers of minerals. In some, each layer is a different mineral. In others, they are different-sized crystals of the same mineral.

Marble
When heat and pressure alter limestone, which is a very common sedimentary rock, marble forms. Impurities in the limestone give marble its many different colors, including red, yellow, brown, blue, gray and green, arranged in veins or patterns.

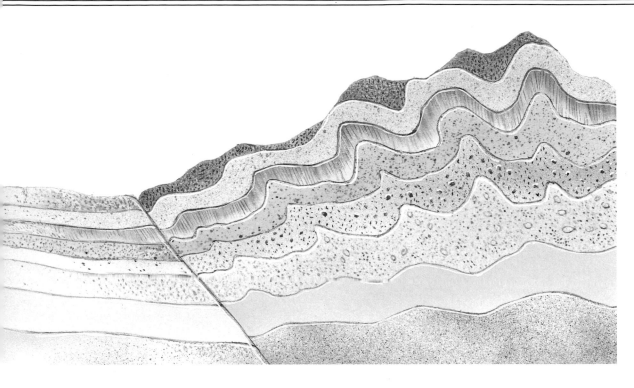

Regional metamorphism

Movements in the Earth's crust can cause rocks to change in many different ways. The nature of the changes depends on the intensity of the pressure and the degree of heat. Slate or schist form at high pressures and low temperatures. For gneiss to form, both temperature and pressure must be very high.

New miningals

Metamorphism causes new minerals to develop in old rocks. The large crystals of garnet in this schist were not in the original rock. The type of minerals that grow depends on the composition of the original rock and the strength of the metamorphism.

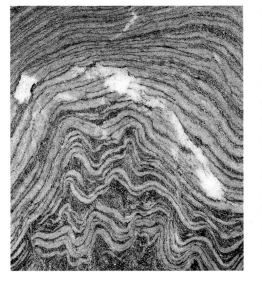

Squeezed almost to melting

When rocks are squeezed and heated, to temperatures close to their melting points, their consistency changes. They are no longer hard, brittle solids that can be cracked—they become plastic (easily molded). This gneiss was deformed when it was in a plastic state.

Why slate splits

The slate from this Welsh quarry will be used mainly for roof tiles. Slate splits naturally into thin slices along lines within its structure. This is because it has been squeezed. Then, small, lamellar (flattened), lined-up crystals grew in layers at right angles to the direction of the squeeze.

GEOLOGISTS AT WORK

GEOLOGY is the study of the history of the Earth, as revealed the rocks found in the Earth's crust. Scientists who study geology are called geologists. Some geologists specialize in certain branches of geology. For example, paleontologists study fossils, mineralogists specialize in identifying minerals and petrologists study the internal structure and composition of rocks.

Most geologists spend some of their time in the field, collecting samples and measuring various features of the rocks that they can see in outcrops. The rest of their time is spent in laboratories, analyzing the samples they have collected and the measurements they have made, often using a computer. Geologists keep detailed notebooks and make records of everything they discover about the rocks in the area where they are working.

The most important record is a geological map. This shows where different rocks may be found, how old they are and whether they are flat-lying, tilted or folded. This information also gives geologists clues about what is going on underneath the Earth's crust. The different rock types are shown on a map in different colors.

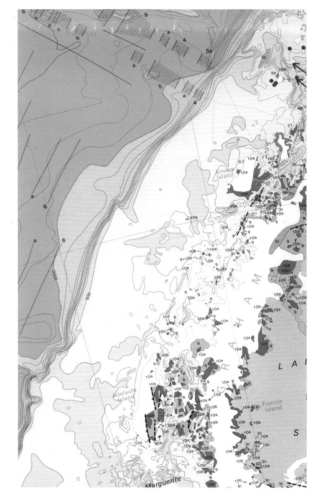

Planning ahead
A geological map is used for many purposes. It is essential in the search for oil and other minerals, and for finding underground water. Architects study a geological map of an area before they plan a building.

Fieldwork
These geologists are sampling water from a volcanic sulfur spring. Most geologists carry out fieldwork like this, collecting various kinds of sample for further study. In this case they will analyze the water to see what minerals have dissolved in it.

Sampling gas
These geologists are collecting samples of gas given off by a volcano. They wear gas masks because some of the gases may be harmful to their health.

Geological hammer

Geologists use a hammer to collect samples of rock. Sometimes they take a photograph of the hammer resting on an outcrop of rock to show the direction and scale of the rock.

FACT BOX

• After rocks have been formed, the radioactive elements in some minerals change into other elements at a steady rate over thousands of years. By measuring the amounts of the new elements, geologists can figure out a rock's age.

• Another way to tell the age of rocks is to look at the fossils they contain. Different plants and animals lived at different times in the past. Identifying fossils can tell you where in geological time a rock fits.

Microscopic photograph

A micrograph is a photograph taken through a microscope. This picture shows the grains in sandstone greatly magnified. Grain size and shape can help to identify sandstones.

Rocks in close-up

Slices of rock are examined under a petrological microscope. This has special filters to polarize light. The slices are cut thinly so that light passes through them. The appearance of minerals in polarized light helps geologists to identify them.

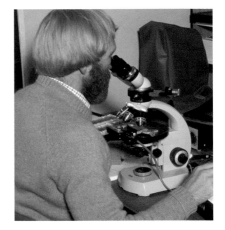

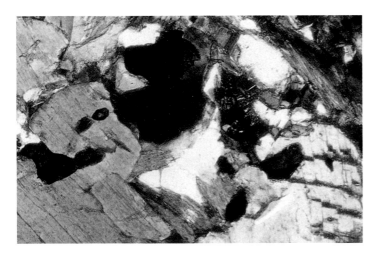

Polarized light micrograph

This micrograph of a thin section of a metamorphic schist was made using a polarizing microscope. It shows the crystals of different minerals that make up the rock. The micrograph helps to identify the rock's origin and the temperature and pressure at which it formed.

Density

These blocks are the same size and shape, but do not weigh the same. The materials they are made of have different densities. Density is used to identify minerals because samples of the same mineral will have the same density.

IDENTIFYING MINERALS

Geologists use many different methods to identify the minerals that make up rocks. Each mineral possesses a unique set of identifying properties. Geologists use several tests to identify minerals, such as hardness (how easily a mineral scratches) and specific gravity (comparing a mineral's density to the density of water). They also look at streak (the color of a mineral's powder), luster (the way light reflects off the surface), transparency (whether light can pass through or not) and color (some minerals have a distinctive color in natural light). Dropping acid onto a sample to see if gas is given off is a simple test that can be carried out in the field. Try these simple versions of two tests that geologists use. They will help you identify some samples that you have collected. First of all, rubbing a rock on the back of a tile leaves a streak mark—the color of the streak can reveal the minerals that are present. Then you can calculate the specific gravity of a sample.

"Acid" test
Drop a rock into vinegar. If gas bubbles form, then it contains minerals called carbonates (such as calcite).

You will need:
white tile, several samples of different rocks or minerals, field guide.

STREAK TEST

1 Place a tile face down, so that the rough side is facing upward. Choose one of your samples and rub it against the tile. You should see a streak of color appear on the tile.

2 Make streaks using the other samples and compare the colors. Rocks made of several minerals may leave several colored streaks.

SPECIFIC GRAVITY TEST

1 Choose a rock and weigh it as accurately as you can to find its mass (weight). The figure should be in grams. Make a note of the mass.

2 Fill a clear measuring cup to the 200 ml mark with water. Now carefully place the first rock sample into the water.

3 Look carefully at the scale on the cup to read the new water level. Make a note of the level of the water in your notebook.

You will need:
mineral or rock samples, accurate scale, notebook, pen or pencil, measuring cup, water.

The mass of a sample divided by its volume gives you its density, or specific gravity.

4 Take the figure you wrote down in Step 3 and subtract 200. This is the sample's volume in milliliters. Now divide the mass (weight) by the volume to find the density. You can use a calculator to do this sum if you want to.

pyrite

beryl

Denser
If a mineral has a specific gravity (SG) of 5, it is five times as dense as water. Pyrite has a SG of 5 and beryl has a SG of 2.6. The atoms in pyrite are more closely packed together, making it denser.

READING THE ROCKS

GEOLOGISTS are interested in what has happened on planet Earth from the time it appeared over 4,000 million years ago to the present day. By reading clues in the rocks they can piece together how the climate changed in the past, how continents moved and how oceans and ice-sheets appeared and disappeared. No single geologist can discover all of this on his or her own. Each individual adds clues that are shared and considered by others in an endless process of detective work.

The first clues come from a careful study of exposed outcrops in the field. What minerals can be seen, and are they crystals? Are the rocks in layers? Are there fossils in them? Are the layers flat or tilted, or bent into shapes like waves? These are just a few of the questions that geologists ask.

More clues come from samples tested in the laboratory. What elements are in the samples? Are the rocks magnetic? How old are they? What kind of fossils do they contain? Each fragment of information is written down or stored on a computer. A store of knowledge about rocks is gradually assembled for geologists, so that they can draw conclusions about Earth's history.

When continents collide
An outcrop of gneiss, like the one above at the surface of the Earth, would tell geologists that the gneiss was once buried beneath high mountains like those on the right. Mountain ranges often develop when moving sections of the Earth's crust have collided, subjecting the rocks to the kind of strong squeezing and heating that creates gneiss. In time, the mountains are eroded away and the gneiss is exposed at the surface. The mountains shown on the right are the Alps, the result of Africa colliding with Europe.

Tropical sea

Limestones like this (left) begin in the sea. Sea creatures play an important part in their development. If you could travel back in time you would find the sea full of strange fish, shells and corals—similar to those in the picture on the right. When these kinds of creatures died, fragments of their shells were then consolidated into limestone.

Strong water

The large, rounded pebbles in this conglomerate outcrop (left) indicate that it came from water with currents strong enough to carry the pebbles. Such sediment could have started on a shoreline like the one on the right, or in a large, fast-flowing river.

Sedimentary basins

On the left, layers of hard sandstone alternate with thinner layers of soft shale, a rock rich in clay. Such sediments were washed into a shallow sea (right) to make what is called a "sedimentary basin." The changes in layers of sediment are caused by changes in the slope of the seabed, the position of the shoreline and the depth of the water.

SEEING INSIDE THE EARTH

How do geologists find out what is deep inside the Earth? Geologists can take measurements at rocky outcrops on land, which provide information about the rocks below. However, only a small proportion of the surface rock is exposed and accessible. Alternatively, geologists may probe down into the Earth. Information obtained from holes made during mining, or from natural caves in limestone areas, shows that the temperature of the Earth increases with depth. Smaller and deeper holes can be made by drilling. Modern drilling machines operate on land or at sea and can collect rock samples from several miles down. They are also able to drill sideways from the bottom of a vertical hole, and this increases the amount of information obtained about rocks at deep levels.

Another way of seeing inside the Earth is provided by geophysics, a sister science to geology. Geophysics is concerned with measuring things in rocks such as magnetism, gravity, radioactivity and the way in which rocks conduct electricity and sound. Three-dimensional maps can be made from measurements that show ups and downs of land. These maps show the distribution and formation of underground rocks.

Vibrating Earth

Earthquakes have helped geologists to understand what the Earth is made of. When they occur it is as though the Earth has been hit by an enormous hammer. The Earth vibrates like a ringing bell. Waves of vibration move right through the Earth. They may be detected on the surface at places far away from the earthquake—even on the opposite side of the Earth. Very sensitive instruments called seismographs are used to measure the vibrations of an earthquake. These have been placed all over the world and are continuously switched on, ready to detect the next earthquake wherever it starts.

Earthquake waves travel at different speeds in different materials and will arrive at the seismographs at different times. All of the seismograph records ever taken show that the core of the Earth is mostly liquid.

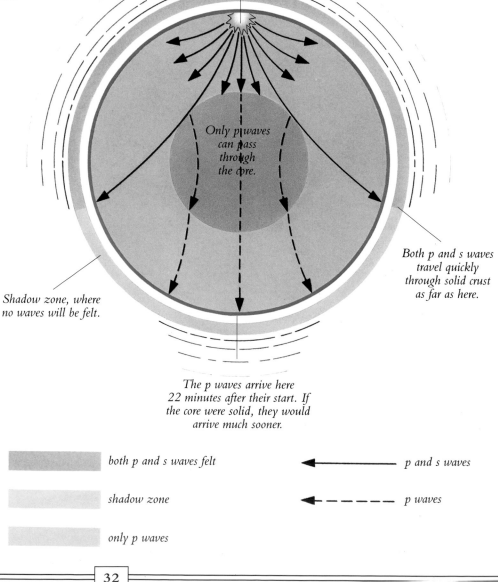

Earthquake starts here and makes vibrations of two kinds—p waves and s waves. The Earth vibrates like a bell, as the waves move outward in all directions.

Only p waves can pass through the core.

Both p and s waves travel quickly through solid crust as far as here.

Shadow zone, where no waves will be felt.

The p waves arrive here 22 minutes after their start. If the core were solid, they would arrive much sooner.

both p and s waves felt

shadow zone

only p waves

p and s waves

p waves

Reflecting sound waves

Bats avoid flying into objects by detecting sound that is reflected from them. Something similar is used to look inside the Earth in seismic reflection surveys. These are commonly done from ships specially designed for the purpose. Loud bangs are made every few minutes by a compressed-air gun towed behind the ship. This sends sound waves down through the water into the rock below. Whenever the sound waves reach a different rock layer, they are reflected back to the surface. The reflections are picked up by a long string of underwater microphones, called hydrophones, also towed behind the ship. Powerful computers analyze the information to read the rocks beneath the seabed.

path of sound waves

hydrophones

airgun

Seismic profile

One of the first things to be produced in a seismic reflection survey is a computerized drawing like the one on the left, showing the reflecting layers. From this, a geologist tries to figure out what rocks are present.

Drilling

Geophysical surveys provide many clues about what lies beneath the ground but they cannot identify rocks. Eventually holes have to be drilled and pieces of rock collected. The holes are made by turning a drill bit, studded with diamonds and attached to the end of a long string of steel pipes. More pipes are added as the bit goes deeper. The samples come to the surface either as broken chips or as solid cylinders of rock, known as core. These men are extracting core from a hole drilled on land.

Handling the data

A modern geophysical survey requires lots of computing power to process information about the inner Earth. This is the computer room in a modern survey ship making a seismic reflection survey. Computers control the airguns on the ship and process the information from each of the geophones.

FINDING BURIED MINERALS

IF we are to use minerals, we must first find them. This is the job of a special group of geologists who are experts in mineral exploration. The task is fairly easy if the target mineral lies at the surface of the Earth, but most surface minerals have already been found. Nowadays, the search is for minerals that are deeply buried and, in some cases, far beneath the seabed. Firstly the geologist selects a promising area, using his knowledge and experience. The area is then surveyed using a variety of methods, all of which depend on the fact that different minerals have different physical properties. For example, rocks rich in iron are magnetic and may be found using an instrument called a magnetometer which measures magnetism. Other instruments are used to measure things such as gravity, radioactivity and other qualities that vary from one mineral to another. In this project you will discover how a simple magnetic survey is done using an ordinary pocket compass instead of a magnetometer.

Using magnetism

This project will show you the principle of the use of magnetism in the search for buried minerals. The Earth itself is a giant magnet. The strength and direction of the magnetism in different parts of the Earth is well known to geologists. In places where the rocks contain a lot of iron, the "normal" magnetism will be changed to a stronger magnetism.

hematite (iron ore)

You will need: *plastic container, clean sand, small magnet, ruler, felt-tipped pens, scissors, stiff card stock, adhesive putty, small compass.*

USING MAGNETISM

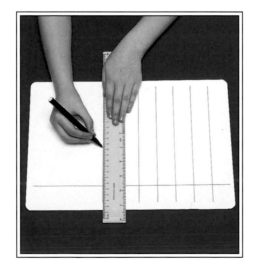

1 Fill a container almost to the top with clean sand and ask a friend to bury a small magnet in it while you are not looking and to level the sand until it is smooth.

2 Measure the container. Cut a piece of card stock to fit inside it. Draw a grid of squares on the card stock. The lines should be about 1 inch apart and parallel to the edges of the card stock.

3 Using adhesive putty, firmly stick the container to the table. Make sure that there are no strongly magnetic items, such as radios, nearby or under the table.

4 Place the compass on one line intersection. When the needle stops moving, hold it down with a finger and make a small dot on the card stock close to the needle's north end.

5 Take the compass away and draw a line from the dot to the intersection where the compass was sitting. Put a small arrowhead on the north end. Repeat steps 4 and 5.

6 Each intersection will now have an arrow coming from it. Most of them point in one direction. This is magnetic north. Put a red dot on the places where they point differently.

7 The dots mark the places where the compass needle was deflected from magnetic north by the buried magnet. They should be grouped together around the same area. Draw a line enclosing each of the red dots.

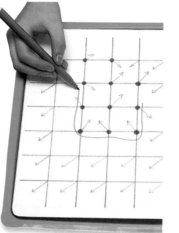

You should have found your "iron ore" buried in the sand.

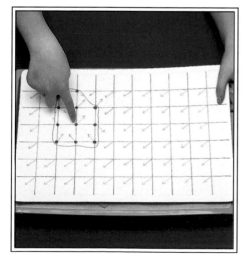

8 Holding your finger above the enclosed area, take the card stock away and leave your finger poised above the place where the magnet lies buried. Dig in to the sand below.

LIMESTONE LANDSCAPES

calcite

flint nodule

The main mineral in limestone is calcite, which dissolves easily. Lumps or layers of flint or chert (forms of quartz) are often found in limestones.

LIMESTONE is a very common sedimentary rock, made largely of a mineral called calcite, which contains the element calcium. Limestone comes in many forms, chalk being one of them. The dazzling white chalk cliffs of southern England are made of limestone.

Limestone forms landscapes unlike others, because calcite dissolves quite easily in rainwater. This causes gaping holes to appear at the surface, which may suddenly swallow rivers and divert them underground. Somewhere downstream, the river will usually come out at the surface again.

Underground, many limestones are riddled with caves formed by the action of the slightly acidic water. Caves may form huge interconnected systems, some of which are still unexplored. Where water drips from rocks inside caves, dissolved calcite is deposited (left behind), forming pillars called stalactites and stalagmites. A limestone rock called travertine forms in the same way, leaving a thick coating much like the kind that forms in a kettle. An extreme limestone landscape called karst occurs where rainfall is fairly high. This is characterized by steep-sided limestone pinnacles separated by deep gullies. China has particularly spectacular karst scenery.

Karst scenery

These pinnacles are in Australia's Blue Mountains. Limestone areas create spectacular landscapes, called karst. Rainwater runs through cracks in the limestone to form underground caves and large holes called sink holes. Where the strata are tilted, deep cracks create pinnacles.

Limestone cones

Cones of limestone rock rise from beside the Li Jiang river near Guilin, China. The strange and beautiful towers were formed by intense downward erosion by rain and river water. The rainfall in this region is very high.

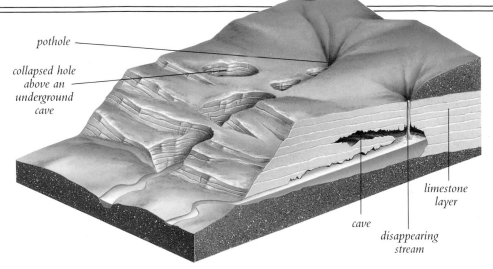

pothole

collapsed hole
above an
underground
cave

limestone
layer

cave

disappearing
stream

Travertine

This famous landscape is the Pamukkale
Falls in Turkey. Over thousands of years,
water from hot springs in limestone
regions has deposited travertine (which
is of the same composition as limestone)
in beautifully shaped terraces. In some
places travertine is quarried and used as
a decorative building stone.

Limestone, the rock full of holes

Rainwater contains acid that dissolves limestone. As rainwater flows over the
surface and through cracks in limestone areas, it slowly dissolves the rock. It
leaves behind holes of all shapes and sizes, including potholes and caves. The
holes have attracted many people who love to explore them. They are called
speleologists (from *spelaion*, the Greek word for cave).

FACT BOX

• Karst scenery covers as much as 15 percent of the Earth's land
area. The word karst was taken from the name of a region on the
Dalmatian coast of Croatia, on the Adriatic Sea.

• In regions where the main type of rock is limestone, calcite
dissolves into the water supply, forming hard water. In hot water
pipes and kettles, some of the mineral is deposited to form brown,
fur-like crystals.

Inside a cave

Stalactites grow down from
the roof of a cave. The drips
that form them also land
on the ground and form
upward-pointing spikes
called stalagmites.
Where stalactites and
stalagmites meet,
a column forms. These
rock formations are
part of the Carlsbad
Caves in New
Mexico.

Limestone pavement

In many limestone regions, pavements with deeply furrowed surfaces
are formed. The furrows, known as grikes, are made by water seeping
through cracks and dissolving the limestone. The blocks of limestone
formed by the furrows are called clints.

ROCK, WEATHER AND SOIL

Black sand

Most sand grains pass through soil at some stage in their recycling process. The sand on this beach is made mainly of the black mineral magnetite. It is formed when basalt, a volcanic lava, is broken down through weathering. It then moves in rivers to the sea where it makes black beach sand.

Peat bogs

The amount of plant material in soil can be very high. Peat soil is made up mostly of dead moss.

Sand dunes

In dry climates where deserts form, sand is blown by the wind to form hills called dunes. These red dunes are part of the Namib Desert in southwest Africa. The quartz grains in the sand were once part of the soil that covered the region when the climate was wetter.

SOIL is another stage in nature's recycling program in which one kind of rock is slowly changed into another. Soil is formed from a mixture of mineral grains, pieces of rock and decayed vegetable matter such as leaves and plants. It forms, by a process known as weathering, when surface rocks are broken down by plant roots and dissolved by water. The action of burrowing animals and insects further helps the weathering process. Some minerals dissolve quickly. Others, such as quartz, are not dissolved but stay behind in the soil as stones.

The soil itself gradually erodes. Particles in it are blown or washed away. There are many different kinds of soil, whose characteristics depend on climate and the type of rock from which they are formed. In hot, wet climates the soils are bright red and thick. In dry or very cold climates the soils are thin or completely absent.

Sea mists provide enough moisture for some plants to survive.

Barkhans are crescent-shaped dunes that are always moving.

The wind creates beach-like ripples on the desert floor.

Soil in layers

Soil occurs in layers, known as horizons. There are four main horizons, called A, B, C and R. The A horizon (also called topsoil) is a layer of fine particles that supports the roots of plants and trees. In the B and C layers beneath the topsoil, the soil particles become larger. The R horizon is partly solid rock.

oak seedling

As trees grow, their roots help break down rock into soil. The roots work into cracks, splitting a rock apart.

Root tips grow down.

Dead leaves

As dead leaves and branches rot they release nutrients into the soil. Trees and other plants need these nutrients to grow.

Beach sand

These grains of sand have been enlarged under a microscope. The sand would have originated in soil—as small particles of rock. Over time, the grains have been transported to the sea.

Graded beds

Sand is moved along by flowing water. Where the current slows, sand and rock particles are deposited. This builds up layers of rock called a graded bed. Movements in the crust can tilt the bed at different angles.

River sand

The particles found in river sand, often of quartz, are generally bigger than in desert or beach sand. They are also more angular in shape. The particles come to rest either on the flood plain of a river or at the river mouth in the delta, where they form gritstone, a coarse type of sandstone.

WHAT IS SOIL MADE OF?

SAND and soil are made of millions of very small particles. Sand is formed from many types of rock, by a process called attrition (grinding down). This usually happens after the grains have been released from a soil that formed in a different place at a different time. Desert sand forms by attrition, as wind–blown mineral grains rub against each other. You can see how attrition forms small particles simply by shaking some sugar cubes together in a glass jar.

Soil is a mixture of particles of minerals, along with dead plant and animal matter. In the first project, a sample of soil is examined, using a sieve to separate particles of different sizes. In the second project, you can find out how graded beds of sediment form in rivers, lakes and seas, as first large and then finer particles of sediment are deposited.

Sugar shaker
Shake some sugar cubes in a jar. The cubes knock together as you shake. After a while you will see many tiny grains of sugar. A similar process occurs in desert sands and on beaches as mineral grains knock against each other and become smaller.

You will need:
gloves, trowel, soil, sieve, paper, magnifying glass, notebook, pen or pencil.

WHAT IS IN SOIL?

1 Put on the gloves and place a trowel full of soil into the sieve. Shake the sieve over a piece of white paper for a minute or so.

2 Tap the side of the sieve gently to help separate the different parts of the soil. Are there particles that will not go through the sieve?

3 Use a magnifying glass to examine the soil particles that fall onto the paper. Are there any small creatures or mineral grains? Note what you see.

BIG OR SMALL?

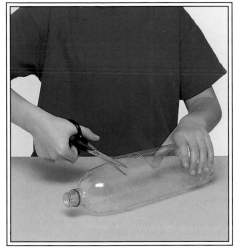

1 Using scissors, cut off the top of a large, clear plastic bottle. Throw away the top part.

2 Put small stones or gravel, soil and sand into the bottom of the bottle. Add water almost to the top.

3 Stir the stones, gravel, soil, sand and water vigorously. In a river, rock particles are combined and carried along by the moving water.

You will need: scissors, large clear plastic bottle, small stones or gravel, soil, sand, wooden spoon, water.

Sedimentary rocks often form in graded beds. This is because particles settle at different rates.

Humus

An important constituent of soil is humus. This is produced by animals called decomposers, such as worms and woodlice. These animals eat dead plant and animal matter, including leaves. As the matter passes through their bodies, it is broken down in their digestive systems.

floating humus and plant fragments

water made cloudy by very fine particles of clay

settled mineral particles

4 Let the mixture settle. You should find that the particles settle in different layers, with the heaviest particles at the bottom and the lightest on top.

PRESERVED IN STONE

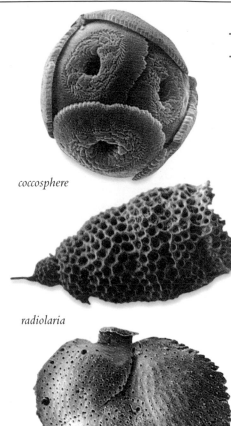

coccosphere

radiolaria

foraminifera

THE remains of some organisms (plants and animals) that died long ago can be seen in sedimentary rock as fossils. After an organism dies, it may become buried in sediments. Slowly, over thousands of years, the sediments compact together to form sedimentary rock. The organic remains of the plants or animals disintegrate, but their shapes or outlines may remain. The hard parts of animals, such as bones and teeth, are preserved by minerals in the rock. Minerals can also replace and preserve the shape of the stem, leaves and flowers of a plant.

The study of fossils, called paleontology, tells us much about how life evolved, both in the sea and on the land. Fossils give clues to the type of environment in which an organism lived and can also help to date rocks. The fossil substance amber was formed from the sticky, sugary sap of trees similar to conifers, that died millions of years ago. The sap slowly hardened and became like stone. Insects attracted to the sweet sap sometimes became trapped in it, died there and so were preserved inside the amber.

Microfossils

Just as there are living organisms too small to see without a microscope (micro-organisms), there are also microfossils. These fossils are tiny marine organisms that lived during the Cretaceous period (about 65 to 144 million years ago). Millions of their remains are found in the sedimentary rock, chalk.

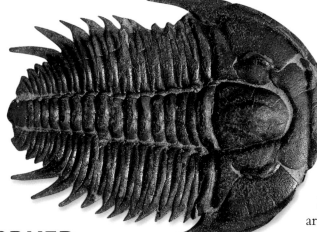

Early animals

Some fossils are the remains of animals that are now extinct. This trilobite, which is 600 million years old, is a distant relation of modern lobsters. Trilobites lived in ancient seas with all kinds of other creatures that are also now extinct.

HOW FOSSILS ARE FORMED

An animal or plant dies. Its body falls onto the sand at the bottom of the ocean or into mud on land. If it is buried quickly, then the body is protected from being eaten.

The soft parts of the body rot away, but the bones and teeth remain. After a long time the hard parts are replaced by minerals—usually calcite but sometimes pyrite or quartz.

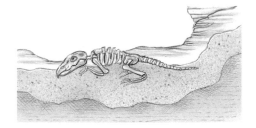

After millions of years the rocks in which the fossils formed are eroded and exposed again. Some fossils look as fresh now as the day when the plant or animal was first buried.

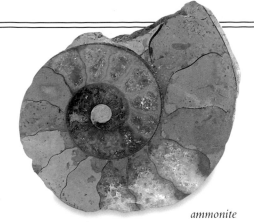

ammonite

amber

Types of fossils

Five common fossils are shown here. Ammonites were hard-shelled sea creatures that lived between 60 and 400 million years ago. Fossils from sea creatures, such as shark's teeth, are often found, because their bones cannot decay completely underwater. The leaf imprint formed in mudstone around 250 million years ago and fern-like fossils are often found in coal. Amber is the fossilized sap of 60 million-year-old trees.

shark's tooth

leaf

fern

FACT BOX

• Perhaps the most interesting fossilized animals are the dinosaurs, that lived between 65 and 245 million years ago. When their shapes are perfectly preserved, expert paleontologists can reconstruct the complete skeleton of the animal.

• Ammonites evolved (developed) rapidly and lived in many parts of the prehistoric world. Because geologists know how ammonites changed, they use the fossils to determine the ages of the rocks in which they are found.

Fossilized crab

This crab lived in the ocean around 150 million years ago. Marine limestones and mudstones contain the best-preserved fossils. Some limestones are made entirely of fossil shells.

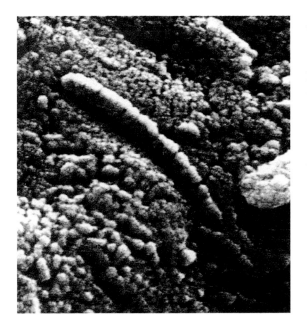

Martian fossils?

In 1996, scientists discovered what looked like tiny fossilized creatures in a rock that had originated on Mars. Everyone was excited about the possible proof that life had once existed on the planet, but it turned out that the marks were probably hardened mineral traces.

MAKING FOSSILS

THESE projects will help you to understand how two types of fossil came to exist. One type forms when a dead plant or animal leaves a space in the sedimentary rocks that settled around them. This is usually how the soft parts of an animal, or a delicate leaf, are preserved before they decay. The space in the rock is an imprint of the dead plant or animal. You can make a fossil of this kind using a shell, in the first project. In this case, the shell does not decay— you simply remove it from the plaster. In another kind of fossil, the spaces are formed when the decaying parts of an animal's body or skeleton are filled with minerals. This makes a solid fossil that is a copy of the original body part. Make this kind of fossil in the second project.

These are the finished results of the two projects. While you are making them, try to imagine how rocks form around real fossils. They are imprints of organisms that fell into mud millions of years ago.

These are a good example of dinosaur tracks. They were found in Cameroon, Africa.

You will need: *safety glasses, plastic container, plaster of Paris, water, fork, strip of paper, paper clip, modeling clay, shell, wooden board, hammer, chisel.*

MAKING A FOSSIL IMPRINT

1 In a container, mix up the plaster of Paris with water. Follow the instructions on the package. Make sure the mixture is fairly firm and not too runny.

2 Make a collar out of a strip of paper and the paper clip. Using modeling clay, make a base to fit inside the collar. Press in the shell. Surround the shell with plaster.

3 Let your plaster rock dry for at least half an hour. Crack open the rock and remove the shell. You will then see the imprint left behind after the shell has gone.

MAKING A SOLID FOSSIL

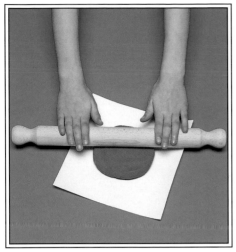

1 Put down a piece of paper to protect your work surface. Roll out a flat circle of modeling clay, about 1 inch thick.

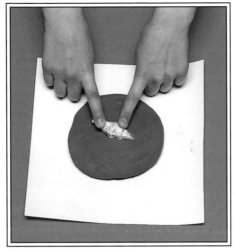

2 Press your shell or other object deep into the clay to leave a clear impression. Do not press it all the way to the paper at the bottom.

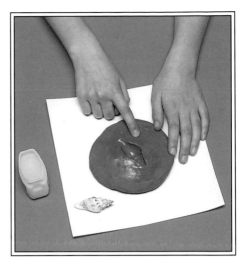

3 Remove the shell and lightly rub some petroleum jelly on the shell mold. This will help you to remove the plaster fossil later.

You will need: *paper, rolling pin, modeling clay, shell, petroleum jelly, paper clip, strip of paper, glass, plaster of Paris, water, fork.*

These jewel-like ammonite fossils were found in England at Lyme Regis, Dorset, a source of many different fossils.

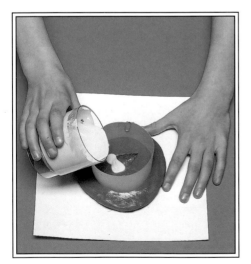

4 With the paper clip, make the paper strip into a collar for the mold. Mix up some plaster of Paris, pour it in and let set for half an hour.

5 Now carefully remove the solid plaster from your mold. In order not to damage them, paleontologists remove fossilized bones or teeth very carefully from rock or soil by cleaning them. They will do some cleaning in the field and the final cleaning back in the laboratory.

USEFUL ROCKS

ALL kinds of things are made from rocks and minerals. Early humans used hard rocks, such as flint, for stone tools. If you look around your house now, you will see many things that were once rocks or minerals. Bricks and roof tiles are made of clay. The cement that holds the bricks together is made from the sedimentary rock limestone. The plaster on the walls may be from a soft, powdery rock called gypsum. The glass in the windows comes mainly from quartz sand. China and pottery are made of clay. Laundry detergent powders and many plastic items come from the liquid mineral oil.

Plastics from oil
Plastics are made from an important group of minerals known as liquid hydrocarbons. One of these liquids, known as ethylene, is hardened through pressure and heat to form the solid plastic, polythene.

ax head

spear head

chopper

spear head

arrow head

scraper

Flint tools
Among the first tools made by humans were stone hand axes and blades. One common material for early tool-making was flint. It fractures easily to give a sharp edge and could be flaked to form many different tools.

The CN tower, in Toronto, Canada, is one of the largest concrete buildings in the world. It is over 1,659 ft high and over 1,400,000 cu.ft of concrete were used to build it.

Reinforced concrete
Concrete consists of aggregate (sand and gravel) stuck together by cement (a mixture of limestone and clay). When reinforced with steel, it can be used for high-rise towers and skyscrapers that would otherwise have been impossible to build.

Crushed limestone
In many countries, limestone is used in larger amounts than any other rock. A layer of limestone, crushed into walnut-sized pieces, makes a perfect base for tarmac on major roads.

lime

soda ash

sand

kaolin

Colored pigments also made from minerals are used as decoration on porcelain.

Making glass

High-quality glass is made by melting pure sand, at very high temperatures. Most ordinary glass is made from a mixture of sand with soda ash and lime, because it melts at a lower temperature. Glass was first made by the ancient Egyptians.

Porcelain china

The most highly prized material for making china is porcelain because it is strong and waterproof. Other ceramics, such as earthenware, absorb water more easily because they are made from coarser clays. True porcelain is made using very fine china clay, known as kaolin.

Marble slabs

Polished slabs of marble make an eye-catching surface for floors and decorative objects. Marble is a metamorphic limestone, valued because it can be easily cut and polished. Some limestones and granites are popular for the same reasons.

building brick

clay

terra-cotta pig

Shaping clay

When clay is mixed with water, it becomes malleable (it can be shaped easily). Clay objects are first molded into shape, then baked in large kilns. Shiny objects are made by coating them with a glaze, which can be made in various colors. Unglazed pottery is called terra-cotta, which is from the Italian word for "baked earth."

FACT BOX

• In the mid-1700s, Coalbrookdale in England became one of the first industrial towns due to its interesting geology. It has an unusual sequence of rocks that includes layers of clay (for pottery and bricks), and coal, iron ore and limestone, which are the essential ingredients for iron-making. Running out of the rocks was natural bitumen, a material that was used to make machine oil. It was also used to waterproof the boats that transported the cast iron.

COAL

peat

Lush rainforest
Damp, swampy rainforest is a similar environment to the one in which coal formed millions of years ago. To produce coal, the remains of plants lay submerged underwater, in swamps or shallow lakes, for millions of years.

T̲HE shiny black material that we call coal is a very useful material. It is called a fossil fuel, because it is from the fossils of dead plants. Burning coal in power stations is one of the ways in which electricity is generated. To most geologists, coal is a type of sedimentary rock made of solid minerals. These originally come from plants that died long ago and became rapidly buried by other sediments, commonly sandstones. Much of the world's coal formed from plants that lived and died in the Carboniferous period, which was between 286 and 360 million years ago. At that time, tropical rainforests existed across Europe, Asia and North America. Coal of a different age is found in India and Australia.

lignite or brown coal

black coal

anthracite

Types of coal
The hardest, best quality coal is called anthracite. More crumbly black coal and lower grade brown coal (lignite) do not give as much energy when burned. Lignite was formed more recently than black coal and anthracite. Peat is younger still. It forms even today.

Coal seams
Coal is found in layers known as seams. The largest may be several yards thick. Between the seams there are layers of sandstone or mudstone. This machine is extracting coals from a seam at the surface.

Bark fossil
This piece of coal clearly shows the bark patterns of the plant it came from. Plants such as tree-like horsetails, primitive conifers and giant ferns grew in huge forests.

Stoking the fire

Coal releases large amounts of energy as heat when it burns. A steam locomotive uses heat from burning coal to produce steam to drive its wheels. The driver keeps the fire well stoked.

Victorian jet brooch

Since the Bronze Age, jet has been carved into many decorative objects. It was popular in Victorian England for mourning jewelry, which was worn in memory of the dead.

Black as jet

Jet is a material that is similar to coal. It is formed from pieces of driftwood that settled in mud at the bottom of the ocean. It is very light and is sometimes polished and carved into intricate shapes.

natural jet

Digging out the coal

In the past, coal was dug from deep underground mines. Today it is mostly taken from large, open pits using gigantic ground-moving equipment. After the coal has been removed the holes left behind are turned into recreation areas. Lakes are created for boating and fishing, and old areas of waste rock are planted with grass and trees. Years ago, this restoration work was not always carried out, so that coal mining areas were unpleasant places to live.

At the coal face

A small amount of coal is still mined underground. Tunnels are built so that people and machines can reach an exposed seam of coal, called the coal face. In areas that are difficult to reach, the coal is mined by hand.

Coal-fired power station

Power stations are often built near coal fields. Coal is used to heat water to make steam. Steam-driven turbines run huge generators that produce electricity.

LIQUID MINERALS

Minerals in rocks also occur in liquid form. Of all the minerals on Earth, one is used by you more than all the others—water. This liquid mineral has greatly influenced the way Earth developed. Without water there would be no oceans, no rivers or lakes, no rain clouds and no plants or animals. The atmosphere would be quite different. It would probably be made of carbon dioxide, similar to all the other dry, lifeless planets in the solar system.

Water is constantly being recycled, moving between the atmosphere, the oceans and the rocks of the Earth's crust. As it moves through the crust, it dissolves, grinds, freezes and thaws, changing the rocks it passes through.

In the oceans, living plants and animals have played a part in the making of another important group of minerals. These are liquid hydrocarbons, from which many essential products such as gasoline, lubricating oils and natural gas are made.

Water supplies
When you turn on a tap you may not think about where the cool, clean water comes from. It may be surface water that has come from a lake or river, or it may be groundwater that has come from deep inside the Earth. Both sources are stopping places in the great cyclic journey made by water. Occasionally water from different points in the water cycle is used. People living on small ocean islands may collect rainwater for their needs. In some countries where rainfall is low, seawater is turned into drinking water by removing the salt.

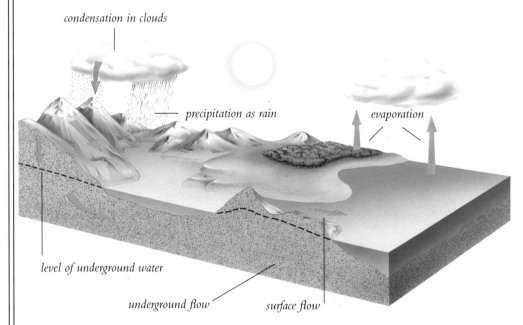

condensation in clouds

precipitation as rain

evaporation

level of underground water

underground flow

surface flow

Water's circular journey
As water moves through its cycle, it changes from water vapor in the atmosphere to drops of liquid rain. Some of the rain falls into rivers and streams that flow into the sea. This water is known as surface water. Some water percolates downward through cracks and pores in rock and becomes groundwater. Sometimes, groundwater seeps out at the surface in springs, but usually it has to be pumped up through wells or boreholes. Throughout its cycle, water slowly reacts with rock and dissolves elements from it. Two types of water are most commonly found, hard water and soft water. The first contains minerals, the second does not.

Clean water
Surface water, such as river water, is often cloudy because it contains particles of sediment such as clay. Water that has not been cleaned at a water plant also contains microscopic matter that can cause disease. Groundwater contains dissolved elements such as calcium and magnesium, but it is clear and sparkling because the rocks it has been filtered through have cleaned it.

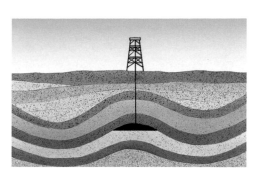

The story of oil begins in warm seas full of living things. As they die, they fall to the sea floor to decay into thick black mud. Unusual events must then occur if oil is to form.

In time, the mud must be buried beneath many layers of sand with clay in between. The sediments must sink deeper and deeper and also become hotter.

After millions of more years, the sediments must come under pressure and fold. Oil from the black mud is then forced into the sandstones and trapped under layers of clay.

From plankton to oil

Liquid hydrocarbons, such as oil, are mixtures of the element carbon and the gas hydrogen. Geologists believe that carbon and hydrogen originally come from small sea creatures known as plankton. When the plankton die, their remains accumulate on the seabed. As they become buried in mud they decompose and make droplets of oil. With time, the mud is buried under very thick layers of sediment. In some situations, the droplets join together to make big underground pools. These get bigger and bigger until they form an oil reservoir.

Extracting oil

Oil reservoirs are often found beneath the sea. Rigs are built over the reservoir to pipe the oil and gas to shore. The rig shown above, in the North Sea, is built on legs that rest on the sea bed. The men who work on the rig are carried to and from shore by helicopter.

The hazards of producing oil

Oil in a natural reservoir is under pressure from whatever is above it. It is usually held in place by a layer of nonporous rock immediately above, which keeps it from seeping away. This is known as the cap rock. When an oil well is drilled through the cap rock into the reservoir, the pressure forces the oil into the well. Strong valves must be fitted to control the flow of oil and turned off when needed. In the well shown on the left, in Kuwait, there was an accident causing a jet of burning oil to rise high into the air. It was eventually extinguished, and the well was made safe again.

METALS FROM ROCKS

AMONG the most important minerals are metal ores. These contain minerals rich in metallic elements, such as iron, copper and tin. To extract the metal from its ore, the ore must first be separated from the rock in which it is found. The ore must then be heated with various other substances in a process known as smelting.

A few metals exist in rocks as a pure element. Gold is the best example and is found as veins and nuggets in many types of rock. Gold is dug from the rock in mines, although in some parts of the world it can be found as grains in river sand. The largest grains are known as nuggets.

Metals are useful to people because they last for a long time. They can also be shaped into many objects or drawn out into a fine wire that will conduct (let through) heat and electricity.

Reclaimed by nature
Metals in the Earth exist joined to other elements. Some quickly rejoin after extraction. Iron quickly rejoins with oxygen and water to form iron oxide, better known as rust.

Gold Rush
Sometimes rocks surrounding a nugget of gold are eroded by a river. Occasionally, the gold is released into the river and can be recovered through a hand-sieving process called panning. This picture shows the 1849 California Gold Rush, when thousands hoped to make a fortune from gold.

Metal sculpture
In many cities you can find statues made of metal. Most are made of bronze, a mixture of copper and tin. This famous statue of Eros in Piccadilly Circus, London, is unusual because it is made of aluminum, a silvery metal. At the time the statue was erected in 1893, aluminum was very difficult to make. It is not easily smelted like other metals and is extracted from the Earth by using electricity.

Fine gold wires
In this close-up view of a microprocessor, you can see very thin wires of gold. Most metals can be drawn into fine wires—a property called ductility. Gold is the most ductile of all metals. It also resists the corrosive effects of many chemicals, making it an important metal to the electronics industry and in dentistry.

stainless steel cutlery

hematite (iron ore)

carbon

Copper

Water pipes and plastic-coated electrical wire are two important things made of copper. The metal is taken from its ore first by removing elements that are not copper. Then it is heated in a furnace with a blast of oxygen.

copper pipes

native copper

Iron

In iron ore, atoms of iron are joined to atoms of oxygen. To produce iron metal, iron ore is heated in a furnace with carbon. The carbon takes away the oxygen atoms, leaving the metal behind. Adding more carbon produces steel, which is harder and less likely to snap or corrode. Steel is the most widely used metallic substance.

bauxite (aluminum ore)

aluminum foil

Aluminum

In aluminum ore, atoms of aluminum are tightly joined to atoms of oxygen. Powerful currents of electricity are used to separate the aluminum from the oxygen.

Smelting iron

Iron ore is heated in a blast furnace to produce almost pure iron. In a process known as smelting, the blast furnace blows hot air through to remove impurities from the ore.

ROCKS AND BUILDINGS

ROCKS have been used for building ever since people discovered ways of cutting blocks of stone from the ground. Stonehenge, in southwest England, is evidence that about 4,500 years ago people knew how to cut, shape and move giant slabs of rock into position. Exactly how they did this is a mystery. In South America, the Incas were building large stone buildings long before the voyage of Christopher Columbus in 1492. All over the world, many examples of stone buildings can be seen. Over the last hundred years natural stone gave way to man-made brick and concrete, but today stone is again being used in buildings.

In the past, builders used whatever rock was common in the area, giving many towns and cities an individual character. For large buildings, the blocks of rock must be free of cracks and natural weakness, and splittable in any direction. They are then called freestone. The best freestones are igneous rocks, especially granite. Of the sedimentary rocks, some sandstones and limestones make good freestone, while marble is the best freestone among the metamorphic rocks. If sandstone splits easily along one direction into thick slabs, it may be used as a flagstone for floors or walls. Slate is a metamorphic rock that can be split into very thin sheets and is ideal for roofing.

The Three Graces
This sculpture is by Antonio Canova, thought to be the greatest sculptor of the 1700s. It is made of marble from Italy and shows the detail that skilled sculptors can achieve using this stone. Polished marble has a special attraction because light is able to penetrate it and is then reflected back to the surface by deeper crystals.

The Taj Mahal
This huge tomb, built in 1400, has an outside surface of white marble that seems to change its appearance in different light and weather. Marble has always been a favorite stone of sculptors because of its gleaming white color. Its fine grain makes it easy to work with.

Roofing slates
Slate is a perfect covering for roofs. It remains almost unchanged by weather and lasts for many years. Slates are made by splitting blocks along natural cracks known as cleavage planes. Today, tiles and plastic have mostly replaced slate as a roofing material. However, it is still used in thick slabs to provide non-slip flooring in large public areas such as airports. The largest slate quarries in the world are in North Wales.

England's earliest stone building

About 4,500 years ago a hard sandstone was used for the largest stones at Stonehenge in southwest England. Like the Incas, the builders managed to shape and lift these very large stones without using metal tools.

St. Paul's Cathedral

After the Great Fire of London destroyed a large area of the city in 1666, the architect Sir Christopher Wren was given the task of rebuilding St. Paul's Cathedral. It took him over 35 years. He chose to build the cathedral using a white limestone from Dorset, England, called Portland stone. Over 6 million tons were used in the new St. Paul's and other buildings in London. The stone was carried in barges along the coast and up the River Thames.

A perfect fit

These stones at the city of Machu Picchu in Peru are of white granite. They were shaped by the Inca people who did not have metal tools. Even now, no one knows how this was done. The blocks fit together so well that a knife cannot be pushed between them. They are even earthquake-proof. The Incas used stone available in the area, such as limestone, rhyolite and andesite.

Walls without cement

In many upland areas where trees do not grow well, stone is used for field boundary walls rather than hedges. They are made with whatever stone blocks can be found near by. Great skill is needed to interlock the different-sized blocks together, without the use of a binding substance, such as cement.

Stone working today

These huge blocks are of white metamorphic marble which is found in the Carrara Mountains of Italy. The blocks are cut from the quarry by drilling lines of closely spaced holes which are then filled with explosive. Carrara marble has a very fine-grained texture and a beautiful luster when it is polished.

ROCKS IN SPACE

*chondrite
(stony) meteorite consisting
mainly of the minerals
olivine and pyroxene*

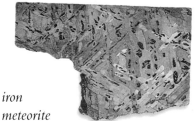

*iron
meteorite
consisting of nickle-iron,
which is strongly magnetic*

*shergottite
(stony) meteorite
consisting of two different
basalt rocks*

Meteorites
There are three main
types of meteorite—
stony, iron and stony-
iron. Stony meteorites
(the most common) are
made of rock. The others
contain nickel and iron.

WE have evidence that rocks and minerals exist on other planets. Other planets and rocky material are in orbit around the Sun. They were formed when the solar system was created, some 4,600 million years ago. Some fragments of the rocky material exists as small particles called meteoroids. Every day, tons of this material hits the top of the Earth's atmosphere. Here, friction causes it to heat up and vaporize, sometimes causing a spectacular display called a meteor shower, or shooting stars. Larger particles do not vaporize completely, and a few actually hit the ground. These rocks are called meteorites.

Some meteorites are from the Moon or Mars. They were chunks of rock that were thrown off the planet when rock fragments from space bombarded the surface, forming craters. The surface of the Moon is littered with craters. When meteorite craters have formed on Earth, they have usually been covered over or destroyed by geological processes, such as the formation of mountains or erosion by the weather.

Meteor crater
This hole in the ground in Arizona is a crater. It was formed by the impact of a meteorite that fell about 25,000 years ago. About six craters of this size exist on earth. Most craters are covered up, filled with water or were eroded long ago.

Craters on the Moon
Many millions of years ago the Moon was constantly bombarded by meteorites that hit its surface, making huge craters. The Earth may once have looked like this. It has few craters today because of the action of wind and rain and movements of the crust that makes up the Earth's surface.

Rocks on Mars

The Pathfinder mission landed on Mars in July 1997. Aboard was a robot probe, called the *Sojourner Rover*, which studied rocks on the surface and sent back photographic images.

Jupiter's moon

This picture, taken in 1979 by the spacecraft *Voyager 1*, shows Io, one of Jupiter's moons. It clearly shows that other planets in the solar system have volcanoes. However, none of the planets is known to have an outer layer that moves over a liquid center, as on Earth.

The red planet

Mars is called the red planet because its surface is covered with red iron-oxide dust. It is the most Earth-like of the planets and may hold important clues for Earth's future climate. Four huge volcanoes and an enormous canyon scar its dry surface.

Asteroids

Many meteorites are thought to be broken fragments formed by the collisions between asteroids (small celestial bodies). Most asteroids orbit the Sun in a belt between Mars and Jupiter. Inside an asteroid is a central core of metal, which is surrounded by rock.

FACT BOX

• Astronauts have brought about 840 lbs of rock from the Moon to Earth. The most common type of rock on the Moon is basalt. It is the same as the basalt on Earth and is formed from solidified lava from volcanoes.

• Only one person is ever known to have been hit by a meteorite. It happened in 1954, in Sylacauga, Alabama. The person was not hurt because the meteorite had already bounced on the ground.

Shooting stars

Meteoroids (small objects from space that hit the Earth's outer atmosphere) travel at high speed. As they pass through our air, they heat up and glow yellow-white, appearing as a bright streak across the sky. This is called a meteor, or shooting star.

STONES FOR DECORATION

Rock paintings
Aboriginal Australians first drew rock paintings like this one thousands of years ago. They used earthy-toned mineral pigments, such as umber (red-brown) and ocher (dark yellow).

raw umber　　*brown umber*　　*yellow ocher*

Pigments
Mineral colors have been used for thousands of years as pigments. Rocks containing colorful minerals are ground down, mixed with a binder, such as egg yolk, fat or oil, and used as paint.

The Millennium Star Diamond
This magnificent pear-shaped diamond from South Africa is one of the finest ever discovered. The hundreds of facets have been cut with great skill to bring out the perfection of the stone. It was faceted to mark the new millennium and is on display in the Millennium Dome in London, England.

MINERALS that are highly prized for their beauty are called gemstones. The main use of gemstones is in jewelry or other decorative work, although some are also used in industry. Around 90 minerals are classed as gems. About 20 of these minerals are considered important gems, because of their rarity. These include diamonds, the most valuable of all gemstones. Some minerals provide more than one type of gem. For example, different types of the mineral beryl form emerald, aquamarine, heliodor and morganite. Gems such as ruby and emerald are distinctive because of their deep color. The different colors of gemstones are caused by metal impurities in the mineral. Other minerals, not necessarily gemstones, are prized for their color and ground down to pigments. These can be mixed with water to make paint.

peridot　　garnet　　moonstone

sapphire

pink sapphire

Jewelry
This necklace is made of gold set with many precious gemstones. Beautiful minerals have been used for thousands of years in decorative jewelry.

Cameo
The gemstone agate occurs in layers of different colors. This makes it possible to carve in layers, using a decorative technique known as cameo. In a cameo, the top layer is carved to reveal the lower one as a background. This Greek cameo is of Alexander the Great.

Specks of pyrite in lapis look like gold.

Lapis lazuli

A mixture of the minerals lazurite, pyrite and calcite forms lapis lazuli. Its blue color is caused by the presence of sulfur in the mineral lazurite. The ancient Persians were the first to crush the rock and use the pigment for ultramarine paint.

natural lapis lazuli

Amber beads

Amber is called an organic gem because it is formed from prehistoric tree sap. Most gem-quality amber comes from the shores of the Baltic Sea.

Blue john is cut and polished to show off the lacy banding.

Jade carving

The characteristic green color of jade comes from atoms of iron metal. Two different minerals are called jade, jadeite and the more common nephrite.

natural nephrite

ruby   *diamond*

Blue john

The distinctive purple banding in the mineral fluorite is commonly known as blue john. In fact, the bands vary in color from purple-blue to yellow. Fluorite is a common mineral and is found in limestones.

natural blue john

Blood and fire

A diamond's fiery brilliance, hardness, purity and rarity make it the most valuable gem. Rubies are rare forms of the mineral corundum. Their blood-red color comes from the metal chromium.

USING ROCKS AND MINERALS

Make paint
Using a mortar and pestle, crush charcoal, brown clay or chalk. Add oil to the powder to make paint.

Many of the materials we use everyday are made from rocks and minerals. Pottery mugs, tin cans and glass windows are just three examples. Many paints, especially those used by artists, are made from colorful minerals. You can make your own paints by crushing rocks in a mortar and pestle.

Gold is one of the few metals that is found in its pure state in nature. It is sometimes found as nuggets in rivers. The nuggets can be separated from mud and gravel by panning, and you can try this in the first project below. In the second project, you can experiment with one of the most widely used mineral materials—concrete.

You will need: *gloves, trowel, soil, old wok, water, measuring cup, nuts and bolts preferably made of brass, dishpan.*

Gold nuggets
A skilled panner can find single pieces of gold in a whole pan of dirt.

PANNING FOR GOLD

nuggets of "gold"

1 Put on gloves and fill a trowel with soil. Place the soil in an old wok, or shallow pan, along with about a quart of water and some small brass nuts and bolts. Combine it thoroughly using the trowel.

2 Swirl the wok around, letting the soil and water spill over the edge. Add more water if any soil remains and repeat until the water is clear. Panning for real gold washes away the mud, leaving gold behind.

3 When the water is quite clear, examine what is left. You should see that the nuts and bolts have been left behind, as real nuggets of gold would have been, because they are heavier.

MIXING YOUR OWN CONCRETE

1 Place one cupful of sand in a bucket. Add two cups of cement and a handful of gravel. Don't touch the cement with your bare hands.

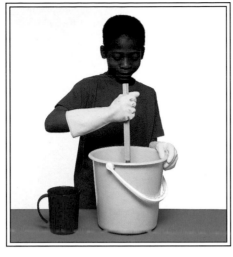

2 Add water to the mixture little by little, stirring constantly until the mixture has the consistency of oatmeal. Mix it well with the stick.

3 Pour the wet concrete onto a tray and spread it out. Let solidify for about half an hour. Wash all the other equipment immediately.

You will need: *gloves, measuring cup, sand, bucket, cement, gravel, water, stirring stick, tray, small thin box, foil.*

hand prints

6 How strong is the concrete block once it has set? Test its strength by trying to bend it. Can you rest a heavy weight on the block?

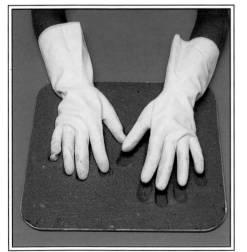

4 At this stage you can shape the concrete any way you want to. Make impressions of your hands, or write with a stick. The marks will be permanent once the concrete has set. Do not use your bare hands.

5 You could make a solid concrete block like those used in the construction industry. First, line a small but strong box with foil. Pour in the concrete and smooth the top with a stick.

GLOSSARY

acid
A class of chemical compounds that contains the element hydrogen combined with other elements. The hydrogen is split from the other elements when the acid is dissolved in water.

amber
A pale brown or yellow transparent semi-precious stone that is the fossilized remains of tree resin. It sometimes contains beautifully preserved prehistoric insects that became trapped in the sticky resin.

ammonite
A sea creature, now extinct, related to modern squids. It lived in a coiled shell now found fossilized in many sedimentary rocks.

anthracite
A variety of hard, shiny coal that burns with hardly any smoke and gives more heat than any other kind of coal.

atom
The smallest part of an element that can exist. It is made up of many other smaller particles including electrons, neutrons and protons.

calcite
One of the most common minerals and the main constituent of limestone. Its chemical name is calcium carbonate.

carbon dioxide
A colorless, odorless gas containing the elements carbon and oxygen that is a part of the air people breathe. It is produced when fuel containing carbon is burned in the air.

cement
A man-made powder made by strongly heating a mixture of crushed limestone and clay. When mixed with water and sand, it sets to a hard solid that is used for building work.

collision zone
A zone on the Earth's surface where the edge of one tectonic plate is being forced into, and under, another. It is marked by lines of volcanoes and strongly distorted rock layers.

compass
An instrument containing a magnetized strip of metal, used for finding the direction of Earth's magnetic north.

crustal plate
Also known as a tectonic plate. One of 20 or so giant areas of rock that make up the Earth's surface.

crystal lattice
The orderly arrangement of atoms inside a crystal that gives the crystal its shape and determines the angles between its different faces.

element
A chemical substance, such as gold, carbon and sulfur, that cannot be further broken down into other elements.

era
A major subdivision of geological time

fossil
The remains, found preserved in rock, of a creature that lived in the past.

geophysics
A sister science to geology concerned with the physical properties of rocks such as magnetism, density and radioactivity.

glacier
A river of solid ice.

gneiss
A common type of metamorphic rock produced deep in the Earth's crust. It is formed when other rocks are subjected to strong pressures and high temperatures.

goniometer
An instrument used to accurately measure the angle between two of the faces on a crystal.

groundwater
Water that percolates downward from the surface of the Earth into spaces in the rocks below.

hydrocarbon
A chemical compound containing the elements hydrogen and carbon.

igneous rock
A rock that forms when magma (hot, molten rock) cools and becomes solid.

impurity
A substance in a mineral or a crystal that is an addition to the normal components and that may cause variations in color. This can happen on the Earth's surface or underground.

iron oxide
A compound (mixture of elements) found all over the Earth that contains both the elements iron and oxygen in various proportions.

karst
A type of scenery found in limestone regions where the rainfall is high. It is characterized by steep-sided pinnacles separated by deep chasms.

lava
Molten rock (magma) that flows from volcanoes or cracks in the Earth's crust.

limestone
A rock, usually sedimentary, formed almost entirely of the mineral calcite.

magma
Hot molten rock in the Earth's interior that is known as lava when it emerges onto the surface in eruptions.

magnetism
An invisible force found in some elements but especially in iron, which causes other pieces of iron to be either pushed apart or drawn together.

metamorphic rock
A kind of rock, such as gneiss, created when the structure of other rocks is altered by intense heat or pressure from inside the Earth.

meteor
A piece of rocky material from space that burns as it falls through the Earth's atmosphere, producing a streak of bright light.

mica
A common crystalline mineral, found in igneous rocks, which splits into thin, flexible, transparent sheets.

micrograph
A photograph taken through the lens of a microscope using a special camera designed for this purpose.

mineral
A naturally occurring substance, found in rocks.

ore
A mineral from which a useful material, especially metal, is extracted.

paleontology
The study of fossils.

pigment
A finely powdered substance used to give color to a material without dissolving in it, unlike a dye.

plaster
Finely powdered mineral, commonly gypsum (or calcium sulfate), which is mixed with water into a paste for smoothing walls inside buildings.

porcelain
A fine, semi-transparent pottery made by firing a mixture of kaolin (a type of clay), and various other ingredients, at high temperature.

quarry
A large, man-made, open hole in the ground from which minerals are taken.

recycle
To convert something old into something new. In nature, old rocks are continuously being changed into new rocks by movement in the Earth.

sedimentary rock
A rock made up of mineral particles that have been carried by wind or running water to accumulate in layers elsewhere, most commonly on the beds of lakes or in the seas and oceans.

seismograph
A sensitive instrument used to detect earthquake waves, from the slightest tremor to powerful shocks.

soil
Material produced from rock, at the surface of the Earth, by the action of the weather, plants and animals.

specific gravity
A number used by scientists to indicate how heavy (or dense) a material is, no matter how large or small the sample.

synthetic crystal
A man-made crystal identical to one found in nature.

Index